THE INTERNATIONAL DRUG TRADE

Nigel Hawkes

ROURKE ENTERPRISES INC.
Vero Beach, Florida 32964

World Issues

Endangered Wildlife
Food or Famine?
International Terrorism
Nuclear Weapons
Population Growth
The Arms Trade
The Energy Crisis
The Environment
The International Drug Trade
World Health

Frontispiece: Inside a hashish den in Pakistan.
Cover: Thai soldier during a raid on opium fields.

Text © 1988 Rourke Enterprises Inc.
PO Box 3328, Vero Beach, Florida 32964

Printed in Italy

Library of Congress Cataloging-in-Publication Data

Hawkes, Nigel, 1952–
        The international drug trade/by Nigel Hawkes.
            p.   cm. – (World issues)
        Bibliography: p.
        Includes index.
        Summary: Focuses on drug addiction and how drugs are produced,
    smuggled, and sold, and what can be done to stop such trade.
        ISBN 0–86592–280–2
        1. Drug traffic – Juvenile literature.   2. Narcotics, Control of –
    – Juvenile literature.   [1. Drug traffic.   2. Narcotics, Control of.
    3. Drug abuse.]   I. Title.   II. Series: World issues (Vero Beach,
    Fla.)
    HV5801.H38 1987
    363.4'5 – dc 19   87–38316
                                                            CIP
                                                            AC

Contents

1
Addiction

The problem of drug addiction is never far from the television screen or the newspaper headlines. We are bombarded with images of hollow-eyed addicts whose lives have been taken over by their hopeless affair with hard drugs: dying in the gutter, or stumbling into court, never seeming able to break away from addiction's grim embrace. These images do not lie. Drug addiction has become a major social problem, and one which particularly threatens young people in their teens and twenties. But it is neither so novel nor, perhaps, so insoluble as television and the press make it seem. Drug addiction is as old as human society itself – but the changes the twentieth century has brought have made it more universal and more threatening than ever before.

Drugs are substances that alter the way the human body works, changing our moods and affecting our behavior. Many of these changes are pleasurable; otherwise there would be little temptation to take drugs, never mind become addicted to them. With some drugs – like caffeine, which is found in tea and coffee – the effect of a normal dose is a barely perceptible "lift" that helps people to do their work and get through the day. With others, like alcohol, the effects are more noticeable. Drinking makes people cheerful, talkative and, sometimes, aggressive; too much of it and even the most hardened drinker will collapse.

Other drugs are even more powerful in their effects, inducing a profound change of mood and a brief ecstatic moment of pleasure. It is easy, though, for users of such drugs to come to depend on them so that they become a permanent part of their lives. Existing without them becomes difficult. Addicts of some drugs deprived of a "fix" shiver, shake and sweat. Their whole purpose becomes that of finding a fresh supply and satisfying their addiction. All other pursuits – work, sports, affection, family life – fall away. Even the basic needs of keeping clean and properly fed are neglected. Honesty is another victim, as addicts are often forced to steal to finance their habit.

Not all drugs, of course, produce addiction of this intense and all-consuming nature. And some addicts are able to live comparatively normal lives. It depends on the personality of the individual. But even these people, who may be counted lucky to survive addiction without destroying themselves, would be much better off free from drugs.

Some dangerous drugs are legal, sold either openly in stores or provided on doctors' prescriptions. Alcohol has existed for at least 6,000

A squalid image of a heroin addict. How helpful are such images in understanding the problem of drug addiction?

years and is so interwoven into Western society that attempts to ban it have always failed. In ancient Egypt, drunkenness became such a problem that half of the breweries were destroyed in an attempt to control it. In the United States, "prohibition" was introduced in 1919, only to be abolished again in 1932 when it was seen to have failed.

Tobacco is a more recent introduction, at least in the West, although there is evidence that the Mayan Indians in South America used to smoke it in long pipes. But it became the basis of a huge industry only with the development of cigarettes at the end of the nineteenth century. Caffeine, which in the low doses found in tea and coffee does not have any ill-effects,

Alcoholism is also a form of drug addiction. Because it is much more common than addiction to the illegal drugs, it is the cause of far more misery and sickness.

has been consumed in China for 5,000 years, though it was only when trade routes were opened up in the seventeenth century that it became known in Europe.

But when people talk about drug abuse, they do not in general mean these legal drugs. They are talking about a range of illegal drugs that cannot be openly sold and used. Some of them, like cannabis, opium and cocaine, are made from plants and have been known almost as long as alcohol and caffeine. Others, like amphetamines, barbiturates, LSD (lysergic acid) and the solvents used in glues and paints, are industrial products that first appeared in this century.

The most common illegal drug in the world today is cannabis, also known as marijuana or hashish. Made from the hemp plant that can be grown widely around the world, cannabis is smoked to produce a feeling of well-being something like that induced by alcohol. Millions of people use cannabis, perhaps as many as 250 million worldwide, in spite of the fact that it is illegal to cultivate or sell it.

More dangerous, and also very widespread, are the drugs produced from the opium poppy – opium, morphine and heroin. Opium is the raw material, extracted as a sticky brown substance from the seed pods of the poppy soon

Wine, coffee and cigarettes – these are all drugs that are acceptable to most people in our society.

after it has flowered. Opium can be smoked in pipes or converted chemically into a more powerful drug called morphine. Originally developed in the nineteenth century as a pain-killer, morphine quickly proved its effective-ness in treating the wounded in the Crimean War and the American Civil War; but equally quickly it became clear that those treated with the drug could become addicted to it.

In 1874, a British chemist found that morphine could be converted into an even more powerful drug, and by the end of the century this was being marketed by the German company Bayer under the name heroin. They sold it as a cough syrup, and it was also used to treat morphine addicts, in an attempt to wean them away from their addiction. Instead, it substi-tuted a yet more powerful addiction in its place. Today heroin is one of the most addictive drugs, with half a million addicts in the United States and similar numbers in Pakistan, India and Thailand. In Britain, there are estimated to be

This man is smoking "crack" – a highly potent form of cocaine that has become increasingly popular in the United States.

about 60,000 heroin addicts, an enormous increase on the figures for the 1950s (when there were less than 100) and even on the lib-erated 1960s, when there were never more than a few thousand heroin addicts.

Another addictive drug whose use has increased rapidly in recent years is cocaine, produced from a shrub that grows in the Andes of South America. For centuries, perhaps for thousands of years, the Indians who live in the bleak regions where the coca plant grows have chewed its leaves, but in the past decade coca has been transformed from a folk remedy to a major international product. As cocaine, it is sniffed up the nostrils to produce a euphoric sensation, and it has become the most fashion-able drug in the U.S., used by the rich and famous with little regard for its dangers.

Cocaine has not yet become as common in Europe or in other parts of the world, perhaps because its effects are similar to those of another well-established stimulant drug usually known to addicts as "speed." Speed is actually a drug called amphetamine sulfate, a white powder that can be eaten, smoked or injected, but which is generally sniffed up the nose like cocaine. Amphetamines were originally developed by chemists as drugs that would enable people to work harder or to manage without sleep. But they are habit-forming and the addict needs larger and larger doses to achieve the same effect. Sometimes they are combined in tandem with a soothing drug like barbiturates in a cycle of "uppers" and "downers" – one to stimulate, the other to calm.

Not all drugs that are abused are necessarily addictive. Drugs that produce hallucinations, like LSD or naturally-occurring "magic mushrooms," do not create addiction. But they may nonetheless be dangerous because they produce powerful and often frightening visions that can cause permanent disturbance in some

Barbiturates, once used commonly as sleeping tablets, are more powerfully addictive than heroin.

people. Usually, however, hallucinogens cause no long-term damage.

The same appears to be true of the bargain-basement form of drug use, solvent-sniffing. The glues, paints and other products that contain volatile solvents are so widely available that it is easy for young people to get hold of them. Some solvents are more dangerous than others, but the main danger is suffocation, which happens when sniffers actually put their heads inside plastic bags containing the solvents. Other long-term damage, to the brain and kidneys, is very rare.

Drugs can be taken in many different ways: they can be eaten, smoked, inhaled, sniffed or injected by hypodermic syringe into a vein. With heroin, injection is the normal technique, although an increasing number of new addicts begin by inhaling the vapor of heroin powder heated on a piece of metal foil with a match or

cigarette lighter – the method known as "chasing the dragon." The widely held belief that it is impossible to become addicted to heroin taken this way is unfortunately untrue.

"Chasing the dragon." This method of taking heroin is less frightening than injection, and so has contributed to the number of people prepared to try the drug.

The 1980s have produced a huge wave of new drug addicts all over the world. Even the 1960s, regarded as a hedonistic, free-for-all decade, produced nothing on the same scale. Yet this epidemic of drug-taking is not unique historically, nor is it inevitable that drugs will continue to spread at the same rate over the next few years. In the past, periods of intense interest in drugs have been followed by periods of reaction in which tougher legislation, combined with a change in attitudes, have brought the problem under control.

During the nineteenth century, opium addiction was certainly much more common than it is today. Opium mixed with alcohol was widely sold as laudanum, a tonic that was used as the cure for a million ills. Sigmund Freud, the founder of psychoanalysis, discovered the pleasures of cocaine and even wrote a book about it. The world's best-known brand name, Coca Cola, was launched as a drink containing cocaine, though it was swiftly removed from the recipe as soon as the dangers of the drug were fully appreciated.

Worse still, throughout the nineteenth century, opium was regarded by the British as a legitimate item of commerce, and two wars were fought by Britain to justify the continuation of the opium trade to China. It was a highly profitable business from which Britain could not be dissuaded by the concerns of the Chinese. Throughout the East, and in the grimy cities of Europe, opium dens flourished in which the customers lay on couches to smoke the drug through long pipes.

By the end of the nineteenth century, doctors had begun to worry about addiction to both cocaine and opium. Cocaine was particularly common in both Europe and the United States, where it tended to be used by those on the fringes of society. If asked, American bartenders would add cocaine to whiskey – just as, in some parts of Britain, you could buy beer spiced with opium to give it more kick.

Antidrug laws began to be passed in the early years of the twentieth century. One of the first was the U.S. Pure Food and Drug Act of 1906. In 1914, forty-four nations signed a convention at The Hague that restricted the production, manufacture and distribution of both opium (and its derivatives) and cocaine. World War I intervened and the Hague Convention was only finally ratified by most countries in 1919, when it became part of the Versailles Treaty. Its effects were hardly immediate: in 1924 a French author estimated that there were 80,000 cocaine addicts in Paris alone. But ultimately, tough new laws, combined with a change in social attitude, were effective. Use of both opium and cocaine diminished so rapidly during the 1930s and 1940s that by the end of World War II hard drug addicts in Europe could be counted in the hundreds. In 1955, for example, there were only fifty-four registered heroin addicts in Britain.

The numbers began to rise again slowly in the late 1960s and early 1970s, as social constraints on many kinds of behavior eased once more. But it was only at the end of the 1970s that a real explosion of drug-taking began. Many people link it to the Iranian Revolution of 1979 that toppled the Shah and sent thousands of Iranians abroad, carrying what little they could with them. One of the most portable forms of property was heroin, easily concealed and then worth a lot of money on the streets of London or New York. But the flood of Iranian heroin brought the street price down dramatically, opening the market to many new addicts. This new, and much bigger, market was then satisfied by new supplies from Central Asia and the Far East.

Today the costs of drug abuse are enormous, both in money and in lives. American estimates published in July 1986 suggest that there are

A source of enchantment, a green spot of fountains and flowers and trees in the heart of a waste of sands.
Samuel Taylor Coleridge on laudanum
Happiness might now be bought for a penny, and carried in a waistcoat pocket.
Thomas de Quincey, Confessions of an English Opium Eater

Right *An opium den in France, 1907. At that time, the use of opium was still legal.*

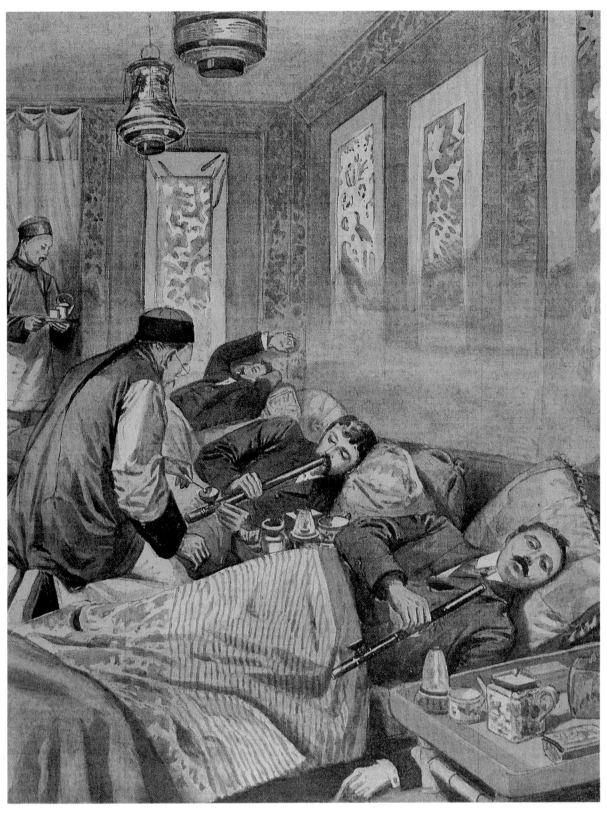

13

4 to 5 million regular users of cocaine in the United States. They spend a total of $25 billion a year on the drug, which averages out to $5,000 per person annually. In comparison, 53 million Americans smoke cigarettes, and their total bill is also about $25 billion a year. This is not to say that cigarettes – or other legal drugs – are not just as deadly as illegal drugs. They are more so, because far more people use legal drugs. But, as high as the cost of drug addiction is in terms of lives and lost dreams, it is still only a fraction of the cost of society's accepted drugs.

Every year, over 300,000 people in the United States die from tobacco-related diseases. Of the drug-related deaths in the United States, 55 percent are from legally manufactured controlled substances, such as prescription pills. Although far fewer people are addicted to illegal drugs than to alcohol or tobacco, use of illegal drugs such as cocaine and heroin is dramatically on the rise, both in the United States and elsewhere.

In Great Britain, the number of people currently using heroin, cocaine or amphetamines is estimated at 60,000 to 65,000. They spend about $750 million a year on illegal drugs, almost the same amount as is spent on over-the-counter medicines like aspirin and cold cures. In other countries, the problems of drug addiction are the same, although there are no reliable figures for how much they spend on their addiction or how many of the users die young. Colombia has 600,000 cocaine users and Peru has 300,000. In the Far East, heroin is the problem: 500,000 users in Thailand, 400–600,000 in India and 11,000 in Malaysia. And these are just some examples.

> All dope can do is kill you – and kill you the long slow hard way. And it can kill the people you love right along with you.
> *Billie Holiday from her autobiography,*
> *Lady Sings the Blues*

A man smoking opium in Thailand, a drug-producing country with huge numbers of addicts of its own.

2
How drugs are produced

In the last quarter of the twentieth century, there are still places in the world where the rule of law operates fitfully, or not at all. It is in these pockets of lawlessness and anarchy that the plants are grown to supply the drugs craved by addicts far away. Anybody that set out to grow the opium poppy in the United States would soon be detected and brought to trial, but in the remote mountains on the border between Pakistan and Afghanistan, and in the Shan States of Burma, the same standards of law and order are not applied.

The opium poppy is a hardy plant that will flourish in poor soil, with little water and no fertilizer. About ten days after the flowers have bloomed, small cuts are made in the plant's seed pods, and a white liquid oozes out. In the air it soon turns reddish-brown and dries to form hard, gum-like balls. This is opium, a drug that has been known for thousands of years. The Greeks and Romans used it, and its name is derived from the Greek word for juice – *opos*. In the sixteenth century, Arab traders carried the plant to the Far East, where it quickly became popular because of its ability, when smoked in a pipe, to produce a feeling of tranquillity and relaxation.

It was a young German chemist, Wilhelm Serturner, who discovered how to convert opium into the more powerful form of morphine. In fact, the process he discovered extracts the active ingredient that makes up 10–14 percent of opium. He called it after the Greek God of Dreams, Morpheus. Today, in secret laboratories, raw opium is converted to morphine by a fairly simple chemical procedure. All the ingredients and equipment are easily acquired, and the procedure does not call for any special skill.

The final stage in the production of heroin is equally straightforward. The raw materials are morphine and a few other readily available chemicals; the product is a bitter-tasting white powder. As a painkiller, heroin is eight times more powerful than morphine, and less likely to cause side effects such as nausea.

The plant from which cocaine is extracted has been in cultivation for just as long as the opium poppy. Its full name is *Erythroxylum coca*, and it is a bush that can grow to a height of more than 9 feet (3 m), though it is usually trimmed back to about 6 feet (2 m) to make it easier to harvest the leaves. It grows along the warm valleys on the eastern slopes of the Andes, at heights of between 1,500 and 6,500 ft (500–2,000 m).

This Thai woman is cutting open the poppy's seed pods to extract the opium.

15

Traditionally, the leaves of the coca plant have been chewed – or, more accurately, sucked – by the South American Indians. Stuffed into the back of the mouth between the cheek and the gum, rather like chewing tobacco, the leaves slowly give up their active ingredients, which are absorbed partly in the stomach and partly through the lining of the mouth. Used in this way, the leaves suppress hunger and anesthetize pain among people whose lives are hard and unrelenting.

Like raw opium, coca leaves contain active ingredients (known as alkaloids) that are

Bolivians gathering coca leaves from terraces in the Andes. The leaves are harvested four times a year.

responsible for their effects. Among these alkaloids the most important is cocaine. It can be easily extracted in a crude form to give a dull white or brownish powder known as coca paste, which is about two-thirds cocaine. Further extractions produce a purer product, which is almost pure cocaine hydrochloride, and this is the product that is smuggled and sold on the illicit market.

16

The third illegal drug produced from a plant is marijuana, which is known by a huge variety of names: cannabis, grass, hash, hashish, pot, reefer, ganja and weed, to list just a few of them. The plant from which it is made is hemp, whose botanical name is *Cannabis sativa*. Like opium and cocaine, it has been known for thousands of years.

The active ingredient in the hemp plant is a substance called tetrahydrocannabinol, which has sedative and hypnotic effects. It is produced in the flowers and leaves. These may be chopped to form a fine mixture and then rolled into "joints" to be smoked. Alternatively, the resin exuded from the flowery tops of the plant may be dried into hard blocks. It is this form that is known as hashish. Hemp will grow almost anywhere, and because no elaborate methods are needed to prepare the drug for smoking, it is by far the most widely grown of the drugs of addiction.

Not all drugs have a history as long as that of opium, cocaine and marijuana. Amphetamines were first created in a Los Angeles laboratory in 1927, and were widely used as stimulants during World War II. It was found that the soldiers given amphetamines could fight for longer without rest, and felt less hunger. After the war, amphetamines were given to depress the appetites of people who were trying to lose weight, in spite of growing evidence that they could cause addiction. Today the prescribing of amphetamines by doctors is much more tightly controlled, and addicts obtain much of their supply from illegal amphetamine production. The chemistry needed to produce amphetamines is not particularly difficult or expensive to organize.

Over the centuries, the opium poppy has been grown in many parts of the world, including Turkey, Iran, India, China, Russia and Mexico. Some is still grown legally to produce morphine and heroin for medical purposes. Illegal production is not fixed; it shifts around

A man harvesting hemp in Colombia. Hemp is grown in most tropical and temperate regions of the world.

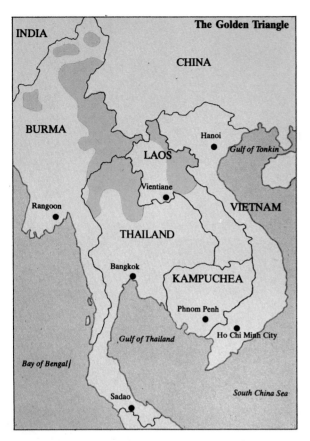

The Golden Triangle

The dark orange on these maps shows the world's major heroin-producing areas. (UAE is the United Arab Emirates.)

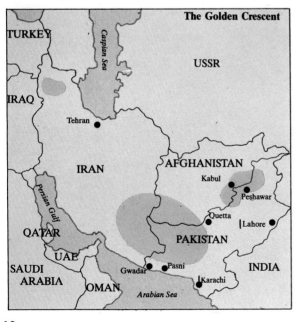

The Golden Crescent

from place to place, as efforts to control poppy cultivation force some farmers to give up. But for the past decade there have been two areas that have supplied most of the heroin reaching addicts – the so-called Golden Triangle, on the borders of Burma, Thailand and Laos in Southeast Asia, and the Golden Crescent, on the borders of Afghanistan and the North West Frontier Province of Pakistan.

Both areas are effectively outside the control of governments. The mountain ranges that run along the Burmese-Thai border are home to a series of private armies, mercenary groups and rebellious tribesmen who are all engaged, directly or indirectly, in the heroin trade. The Thai government permits this situation to continue because it sees this no-man's-land of warring groups as a useful buffer between Thailand and the neighboring states to the north and east. In fact, the rival factions are so well armed that it is far from certain the Thai army could clean them out even if it wanted to.

The politics of the North West Frontier of Pakistan are more traditional. This area is the home of Pathan tribesmen who have a fearsome and well-deserved reputation as warriors. No conqueror since Alexander the Great has managed to subdue them for long; and for the past decade it has proved beyond the capabilities of the government of Pakistan.

A principal reason is the war that has been going on over the border in Afghanistan since 1979 between the Soviet Union and the Afghan guerrillas. Huge supplies of light arms have been poured into the area by Western nations who support the Afghan cause. Many have got no further than the border tribesmen, who prize weapons above almost any other possession.

It is possible to drive up the major road that leads from Peshawar over the Khyber Pass to Kabul, the capital of Afghanistan. The road is dotted with impressive fortresses once occupied by the soldiers of the British Raj and now by Pakistan's Khyber Rifles. They are well trained and led, but they do not really control the bare gray mountains that rise on either side of the road. As soon as you leave the road you are in the territory of the Pathans, who have discovered that the opium poppy is by far the most profitable crop to grow on their stony land.

In this area the average landholding for a family is around a fifth of an acre. Only two crops will grow: wheat or poppies. If wheat is grown the income is about $20, but the poppy will yield about $600. It is easy to grow and harvest – so it takes little imagination to work out which crop the tribesmen prefer.

> Heroin is our mineral wealth.
> *Anonymous source, North West Frontier Province, Pakistan*

As the poppy flowers begin to fade, the harvest begins. The raw opium oozes from fine slits cut in the central seed pod, hardening as it is exposed to the air. It can then be scraped off and collected in bowls. The egg-sized pods or capsules can be cut repeatedly, but the opium content of the fluid decreases each time. Once collected, the opium hardens and can be formed into balls, to be carried by hand or on

The Khyber Pass leading from Pakistan to Afghanistan. This barren, mountainous land produces much of the heroin on the world market.

the back of a donkey to the market for sale. At Landi Kotal, a dust-blown town at the head of the Khyber Pass, raw opium is sold openly in the bazaars alongside rifles, daggers and bandoleers of ammunition.

The farmers who grow the crop do not get rich. Although the heroin trade is a huge business, most of its profits are cornered by middlemen. As Professor Sayyid Jafree, president of the Pakistan Constitutional Law and Public Interests Center in Lahore, puts it: "The farmers of the North West Frontier have been cultivating poppies since time immemorial, but they are eking dismally little survival out of it." The profits, he says, are made by others, people with perfectly respectable fronts who have become millionaires over the past two decades – thanks to the heroin trade.

19

Almost exactly the same is true of the poor peasant farmers who grow coca in Latin America. Like the poppy growers, they find coca is a more profitable crop than any alternative, but few actually grow rich by cultivating it. It has, however, become a major factor in the economies of Peru, Bolivia and Colombia.

In Peru, for example, up to 250,000 acres of land in the Huallaga valley are believed to be planted with coca bushes. The leaves are harvested four times a year, with each acre yielding about 100 pounds of leaves, which are converted into coca paste by barefoot workers who trample the leaves rather like the old-fashioned treading of grapes to produce wine. Small producers can make far more by cultivating coca than any other crop, and the chewing of the coca leaf is so firmly embedded in the society of the high Andes of Peru and Bolivia that eliminating it is probably impossible.

The conversion of coca paste to cocaine has traditionally been carried out in Colombia, though there is growing evidence that it is also occurring today in Peru and Bolivia. Crude laboratories buried out of sight of the authorities in jungle clearings produce cocaine of various degrees of purity for smuggling on to the major markets in the United States. Narcotics experts believe that there may be up to three dozen laboratories in Bolivia today, with the capacity to process much of the 32,000 tons of coca leaves harvested each year. About one person

Right *In Bolivia, the coca leaf is thought to have magical properties. These Chipaya Indians are using the leaves to predict the future.*

Below *After harvesting, the coca leaves are dried in the sun before being trampled to a paste in trenches of paraffin.*

in twenty in Bolivia is now involved in either growing or processing coca, and the business is reckoned to yield some $600 million a year in export earnings – more than the total for all legitimate exports. Peru's coca trade is said to be worth $1 billion a year, against a total for all other products of $3 billion.

No comparable figures exist for the illegal production of drugs like amphetamines and LSD in the West, though the amounts are probably substantial. And a totally new business is just beginning to emerge in the production of the so-called designer drugs, synthesized chemically in sophisticated laboratories and designed to reproduce the effects of substances like heroin.

An example is a chemical called 3-methyl fentanyl, derived from a widely used anesthetic. It is said to produce an effect similar to that of heroin, but much more intense. A skilled chemist can produce the drug with equipment that would cost around $2,000, a trivial sum compared with the possible returns. So far, the drug has been found only in California, but the potential for such synthesized drugs is enormous. One major advantage for the producers is that such drugs do not appear on lists of banned substances, so producing them is legal.

A jungle laboratory for manufacturing cocaine in Bolivia. The process involves treating coca paste with various acids.

3 Smuggling and trafficking

Some of the most ingenious criminal brains in the world have devoted the past decade to the task of smuggling heroin, cocaine and marijuana from the places where they are produced to their final markets in the West. The smugglers have several things on their side. Heroin and cocaine are, weight for weight, about the most valuable commodities available: very small amounts, which are easy to conceal, are worth large amounts of money on the street. Nor is there any uncertainly about the market – drug addicts are the most reliable customers

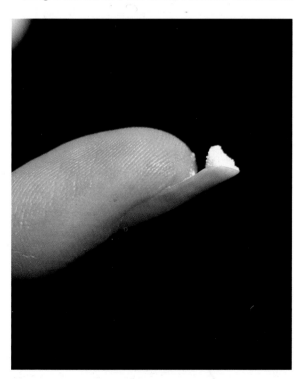

A single gram of cocaine would be worth around $100 in the United States.

it is possible to imagine. Better still, many addicts are so desperate for money that they are prepared to undertake the riskiest parts of the enterprise themselves, while gaining only a tiny fraction of the rewards.

Like any conventional form of trade, the drug business involves producers, middlemen and retailers. It is the middlemen who set up the deals, finance the trafficking and pocket most of the profits. While the farmer who produces a conventional product such as milk can expect to receive somewhere between a third and a half of the final price paid by the consumer, the peasant farmers who grow opium poppies in the Golden Crescent would be lucky to get one-twentieth of the street value of the drug. The final retailers – generally dealers in a small way who are themselves addicts and use dealing as a way of financing their own habit – are equally the victims of the system. Few of those who actually sell small packages of heroin on the street for $10 and $20 a time make any real money. Their risks are large, and their rewards are small.

Equally victimized are the couriers whose job it is to smuggle drugs through customs checks. For payments of between $5,000 and perhaps $10,000 a trip, they shift consignments of drugs worth millions of dollars on the street. If caught, they risk jail and, in some countries, the death penalty. Yet they are comparatively small fry, their greed for easy money exploited by others.

The routes taken by drugs on their way to the rich markets of the developed world change constantly. But for the past ten years, they have had common starting points in the heroin- and cocaine- producing areas of Southeast and Southwest Asia and Latin America.

Today most opium is converted into heroin close to its point of production. Heroin is both more profitable and easier to smuggle. In Burma, the main heroin producer is believed to be Khun Sa, a warlord in the Shan States who commands his own private army. He buys the raw opium from the producers, converts it into heroin, and then sells it on to a group of Chinese traders who operate in the towns of Chiang Mai and Chiang Rai in northern Thailand. These families are rich, successful and also trade in legitimate commodities like rice or televisions. Unlike Khun Sa, they are never publicly identified with the drug trade; they operate discreetly and invisibly. They sell the drug on to other Chinese traders, who distribute it around the world through a tight network of families. There is no paperwork for these transactions. They are done on the basis of a

Khun Sa is the world's biggest drug dealer. He presides over a private army in the Golden Triangle where the authorities do not dare to challenge him.

handshake, and any money is always paid in another country, so there is no evidence that any deal has been done.

The networks that carry the heroin out of Pakistan are less clear-cut. Some finds its way down the main highway from Landi Kotal through Peshawar to Lahore and Karachi, concealed in the cargo of the brightly painted trucks that use the road for legitimate trade. There are supposed to be 200 police checks along this road, but with hundreds of trucks passing every day it is impossible to check them all. Other consignments are smuggled

A bus coming down the drugs route from Afghanistan to Pakistan. Buses and trucks on this road are often used to smuggle heroin.

over the border into India and find their way overland to Bombay. Although India is not believed to be a major source of illicit heroin, it is one of the principal smuggling routes for heroin produced in Pakistan and Afghanistan. The traders are Asians who use the same kind of family networks as the Chinese to distribute the product to the West.

For the drug traders, the most dangerous part of the operation is transporting the drug by air or sea from Asia or Latin America to Europe and the United States. For this task they employ couriers, people who for a few thousand dollars are prepared to run the risk. Almost anybody may be a courier: flight attendants, diplomats, soldiers, old-age pensioners,

beauty queens, a Pakistani squash champion and a Japanese Boy Scout have all been caught trying to carry drugs. Women hired as couriers will sometimes carry babies with them to allay suspicion; some have even taped packages of heroin to the baby's body, or concealed it in cans of powdered milk or a baby's bottle.

Many techniques have been used to conceal the small packages of drugs. One smuggler sent a cargo of live parrots to London. When they arrived, two appeared to have died in transit – but in fact they had been killed, gutted and stuffed with cocaine. Another smuggler dissolved cocaine and impregnated his clothes with it. At the other end he planned to extract the drug again by dissolving it out in boiling water. Yet another sent a cargo of crocodile skins, which are normally covered with talcum powder to protect them in transit. This time the powder was not talc, but cocaine.

A common technique is to pack balloons or condoms with drugs and then swallow them. At the other end, after the courier has passed through customs, nature will take its course and the condoms will pass through the body to be recovered. Couriers who use this method are known as "mules" or "camels." They practice by swallowing whole grapes or olives, progressing by stages to large objects like onions. It is a very dangerous method, for if the condoms burst inside the stomach, death will follow. In June 1986, Masoud Mirshani, a carpet importer from Teheran, died when eighteen of the forty-five small balloons he had swallowed burst.

More obvious methods can also work, for the volume of passengers and cars passing through the ports and airports of the West is so enormous that it is impractical to check more than a small minority of them. In a recent trial of a

A foreigner was caught in Thailand after swallowing fifty of these condoms packed with heroin.

group of Italian drug smugglers, it was revealed that they had hidden marijuana and heroin inside hollowed-out pieces of furniture.

First they imported marijuana worth about $1.3 million inside a consignment of desks made in Kashmir and sent by container to England. Later they tried the same trick with 132 pounds of heroin, hidden inside furniture made in Thailand. In each cash the smugglers, although based in Britain, intended the crates to finish their journey in Canada, where the heroin is worth much more. Canadian customs officers would have been less suspicious of furniture that had apparently been sent from England.

The smugglers are aware that customs officers are more likely to be suspicious of travelers or cargo arriving from known drug sources, so they try hard to conceal their tracks. Spain has become a major center for the trade, with cannabis from North Africa and cocaine from Latin America arriving there to be smuggled on to Britain concealed in the cars or the luggage of returning vacationers.

A drug-smuggling network was uncovered in Finland when officials found marijuana hidden in the hollowed-out pages of books.

Once the drugs are past customs, the final stage in the distribution begins. The popular image of "pushers" relentlessly persuading people to try drugs for the first time is not an accurate one, according to the police. Of course there are major dealers at the center of the network – many of them involved in a whole range of different crimes in addition to drug trafficking – but actually appearing openly to sell their wares would be far too risky. They depend instead on young people acquiring the habit from their friends, at a party or in a group. Curiosity – just trying once to find out what it's like – is probably most addicts' first experience of drugs. Many never progress further, but those that do become addicted and quickly learn where to obtain supplies.

Drug users buy their supplies on the street, or in a bar or other meeting place, from people they know. The sellers are often only dealers in a very small way, providing drugs as an act of friendship and a way of financing their own habit rather than as a way of making money. They in turn get their supplies from a close-knit network often based on family or national ties. There are, for example, Asian networks that distribute the heroin in Britain, while in the United States organized crime in the form of "Cosa Nostra" – the Mafia – has been heavily involved. Colombian networks are closely involved with the cocaine trade.

Violence is part of the stock-in-trade of those who profit from drugs. In Sicily at the height of the Mafia's power in the early 1980s, it took real courage to become involved in the battle against them. In April 1982, General Dalla Chiesa was appointed Prefect of Palermo, Sicily's main city, and declared war on the drug

Left Defendants behind bars in "the bunker" – a huge, fortified courtroom – during the Mafia trials in Palermo in 1986.

traffickers. Five months later, he and his wife were gunned down. Two prominent judges were also killed. Battles between rival Mafia "families" claimed many lives. Finally, public disgust erupted, and the Italian government launched a major effort to jail Mafia leaders.

The Colombian drug traffickers have also used violence in an attempt to suppress opposition. The Minister of Justice was murdered. So were more than fifty magistrates and judges, and the editor of *El Espectador*, who had campaigned against the trade. In early 1988, they kidnapped and killed Colombia's Attorney General, who was working with the United States to extradite drug traffickers to the U.S. for prosecution. The kidnappers call themselves "The Extraditable Ones" and have waged war on anyone who dares to come after them. Colombia's average citizens are as against the drug trade as anyone else; in 1987 over 50,000 young people participated in marches against drug use and trafficking.

United States officials say Colombian traffickers control 80 percent of the cocaine entering the United States.
New York Times

Drug dealing can be very profitable. In Pakistan, 1 kilogram (2.2 pounds) of heroin costs $7,000 or less. Once in the United States, that heroin may pass through as many as seven different dealers, each of whom will dilute the heroin with milk, sugar, quinine, cornstarch, or almost any white, powdery substance. The resulting mixture may contain as little as 1 to 2 percent heroin. This mixture is sold in glassine packages or in larger rubber balloons containing 350 to 400 milligrams, which is less than half a gram (.0325 ounces). Each bag or balloon costs from $10 to $25, depending on its purity and where it is purchased. All told, the original

Guns and drugs. This submachine gun and ammunition were taken with bales of marijuana in a raid by the Miami drug squad.

kilogram will eventually yield as much as $250,000.

These figures, though rough and ready, give some idea of where the big profits are made. The farmers, as we have seen, do better by growing poppies than any alternative, but do not get rich. The retailers enjoy a normal markup of 100 percent – profitable but not extortionate. The real money is made by the traders who buy the drug at its point of origin and contrive to smuggle it to the final market. They could make even more if they sold it directly themselves, but the risks are too great. From their profits they have only to pay the couriers – but a fee of $5,000 is little enough compared with the value of the cargo smuggled, which could easily be $200,000.

4
Stopping the trade

Throughout the West, governments have declared a war on drugs. But it is a war that is proving difficult to fight; a war in which the enemy is hard to identify and even harder to catch. At present, most experts agree, it is a war that the West is losing. At least 90 percent of the drugs smuggled from Asia and Latin America reach their destination untroubled by the activities of police or customs officials. The amounts that are intercepted are a very small proportion of the total.

The reasons are not hard to understand. The vast majority of the heroin destined for the United States arrives by commercial air, or in other words, on regularly scheduled airline flights. Each year, 19 million people fly in and out of JFK, New York's international airport. Millions of other air passengers use international airports in Miami, Los Angeles, Chicago, Seattle and many other U.S. cities. Although in the past few years drug enforcement officials have seized an increasing number of drug shipments sent by air, they cannot detect and catch them all. Most of this heroin has been shipped from Southwest and Southeast Asia.

Heroin and other drugs from Latin America often come by land across the U.S.-Mexican border. Two thousand miles long, this border is controlled only at border towns, where U.S. Customs officials secure ports of entry. For all the drugs seized at the border, many escape detection.

In the past, some success has been achieved by cutting drugs off at their source. Turkey, for example, was once a major supplier of heroin but was persuaded to clamp down on the trade in the early 1970s after President Nixon brought pressure to bear. But today's main sources of drugs will probably not respond to the same

pressures. The Pakistani government, a close ally of the United States, has made some efforts to reduce the growing of opium poppies and has published figures that claim to show that the production of opium in the North West Frontier Province has declined from a peak of 800 tons in 1978–79 to no more than 40 tons by the mid-1980s. Many observers doubt the accuracy of these figures, since the supply of heroin to the West appears to be undiminished. The Pakistani government's reply is that production has now moved over the border into Afghanistan and out of its control. This may well be partly true.

Cars waiting to board a passenger ferry. Any one of these vehicles has numerous hiding places for drugs and they cannot all be searched.

The situation on the Burmese-Thai border is equally out of control. Much of the opium is grown on the Burmese side, where the government turns a blind eye, and on the Thai side, where the trade routes begin, local warlords and remnants of the old Chinese Kuomintang army rule the roost. When the Thai army has attacked the supply chains of Khun Sa it has been beaten back.

In any case, the business is now so large that some governments are reluctant to take action. To appease pressure from the U.S. they will pass laws restricting the growing of coca or opium poppies, but enforcing those laws is another matter. Even when governments are

"Get the Mafia out of the customs" says this graffiti in Bolivia. However, the generals and landowners who profit from the drug trade are powerful opponents of reform.

willing, their public servants are often weak. In poor countries, where customs officers and policemen earn barely enough to keep their families alive, bribing some of them to turn a blind eye is not difficult. In Pakistan, a number of senior officials have been implicated indirectly in the drug trade; and although many know the names and addresses of those controlling the trade, nothing is done to bring them to trial. Exactly the same is true in Colombia.

31

Malaysian fishing boats are known to be involved in drug running, but the long coastline is impossible to survey effectively.

Western governments have therefore been forced back to the traditional method of customs inspections at ports of entry in an attempt to control the inflow. Random inspections are still carried out, but they are not very effective. To search more than a fraction of the cars and passengers moving in and out is impossible: thousands of inspectors would be needed, and there would be long delays for passengers at ports and airports. Much more sophisticated methods are needed, including better intelligence about travelers likely to be carrying drugs, and better methods of detecting the consignments as they enter the country.

Without information, searching for drugs is like looking for the proverbial needle in the haystack. To provide this information, Western governments are now basing officials known as Drug Liaison Officers at their embassies abroad. The Americans, West Germans and British all have such officials in Pakistan and,

while for obvious reasons the intelligence they provide is not made public, they are thought to do a useful job. Recently India has agreed with some reluctance to allow Britain to post two such officers there to monitor the traffic through New Delhi and Bombay.

Ordinary police work at home can also provide clues. Bank managers suspicious about sudden deposits of large amounts of cash may pass on their doubts to the police. In the United States, banks have a legal obligation to report all cash deposits greater than $10,000, though this is not very effective. Its result has been to encourage sophisticated "money-laundering" operations in which the profits from drug dealing are concealed by passing them through foreign banks and the accounts of legitimate companies.

Sometimes drugs barons give themselves away by an abrupt change in their standard of living. One Englishman, ringleader of a gang who smuggled heroin through the London airport hidden in girdles, moved from a small apartment in North London to a $250,000 house in the country, acquired two expensive cars, flew by Concorde and stayed in the best hotels abroad. He could hardly have done more to draw attention to his changed circumstances.

Often police and customs officers have much more fragmentary evidence to go on. An agent may get a tip from a contact that a drug run is planned, but without sufficient detail to be certain of intercepting it. In the United States, the Customs Service is using several different techniques to improve its ability to stop the flow of drugs into the country. It has expanded its intelligence effort, working with Drug Enforcement Agency officers in other countries and adding intelligence officers in all the regions of the United States. In 1986, the intelligence branch in the northeast region of the United States provided support to a major cocaine air smuggling investigation, which resulted in indictment of twelve people who were charged with smuggling a total of 7.5 tons of cocaine worth $25 million over a five-year period. Approximately $7.3 million was seized as a result of this investigation.

The customs department is also designing state-of-the-art equipment to detect drugs in various situations. For example, mobile X-ray systems, set up in vans, are currently being tested for primary use at airports on bulk cargo and baggage. At several customs locations,

A suspicious sample is analyzed by the Thai Narcotics Bureau. Purple is positive for heroin.

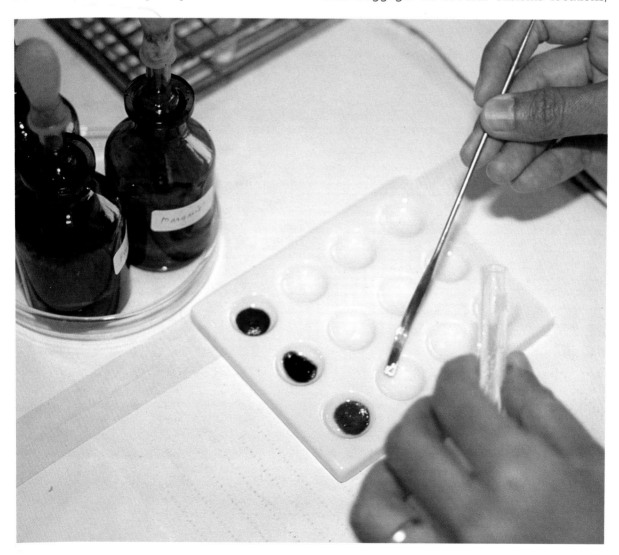

fiberscopes have been tested; these portable instruments have proved to be very useful tools for examining car doors, gasoline tanks, and other hard-to-inspect locations in search of contraband. Nuclear magnetic resonance technology forms the basis of a system that allows the rapid screening of letter mail in search of cocaine, heroin and morphine.

Another high-tech aid has been the automatic license plate reader, which uses optical character recognition techniques, an automatic TV camera and a microcomputer to locate, read and enter license plate data into a computer to verify the information. This device was first tested in 1986 at a port of entry on the Mexican-U.S. border.

Dogs tained to detect the scent of drugs have been very useful and have had a high success rate. There are now over 160 canine teams in the field nationally. So far, attempts to produce an artificial "sniffer" to match the acute sensitivity of a dog's nose have failed. One interesting item introduced recently is a cannabis detection spray. This chemical causes marijuana to change color.

The quantities of drugs intercepted by customs officers in all Western countries is rising, but it is unlikely that this reflects better detection methods. It is more likely that they are detecting the same proportion of a rising total, as drug addiction grows and the traffickers increase their shipments.

It is impossible to guess what proportion of

Dogs are useful in situations like this one where a car has entered Britain by ferry.

the total amount of drugs being smuggled into the country is detected; the best estimates are between 5 and 10 percent. Over 24 million people fly into the United States from outside the country every year and pass through customs; customs officials cannot possibly inspect every piece of baggage.

Seizures, of course, are not the whole story. If drugs are seized from couriers but the rest of the network left in place, little is achieved. One technique that is widely used is to search baggage before it is sent through to the baggage claim area. If drugs are found, they are removed and replaced with substitutes. Then the courier is deliberately allowed to pass through customs and followed to the handover point. In this way more members of the network can be rounded up and, under questioning, they may reveal further names and contacts.

The problems American authorities face are particularly vast. In 1986, government officials estimated that 150 tons of cocaine, 12 tons of heroin and up to 65 tons of marijuana would be smuggled into the United States, and that 90

American customs boats patrol the coast of Florida, hoping to intercept drugs arriving from Latin America and the Caribbean.

percent would get through undetected. Much of the smuggling takes place across the 1,864-mile (3,000-km) border with Mexico, where the smugglers have built their own airstrips for landing light planes. Southern Florida is also a major entry point for boats and light planes, some of which reach the United States via small islands in the Caribbean.

But as soon as pressure is applied in one area, the smugglers shift their attack, moving to the Atlantic coastline of North Carolina, Virginia and Delaware, and to the Gulf of Mexico. The methods used are sometimes bizarre. One smuggler – actually a former police drug agent – tried to parachute into rural Tennessee with 73 pounds (33 kg) of cocaine strapped to his body. He would probably have got away with it if his parachute had functioned properly, but he died in the jump.

In keeping with President Reagan's intention

to fight a war against drugs, the United States has used its armed forces in a series of operations against drug traffickers. In 1984 and 1985, the U.S. Navy mounted blockades in the Caribbean designed to catch drug runners' boats. In 1986, U.S. Air Force helicopters were used to carry Colombian police in a raid on a heroin and cocaine factory in which twenty people died. Air Force planes have also been used to transport Bahamian security forces to remote islands used by traffickers. The U.S. Air Force has even positioned a radar balloon in the Bahamas, with a second in Florida, to try to keep track of aircraft movements – many of which are illicit drug runs.

The boldest move so far came in the summer of 1986, when six helicopters and several transport planes carrying 160 men joined Bolivian forces in a massive attack on the drug-producing areas of Bolivia. The idea was to wipe out about three dozen laboratories where coca leaves were processed into cocaine.

The raids appear to have been less successful than had been hoped. There was evidence that many of the drug traffickers had had

There is big talk about a war against drugs, but it is a war being fought without a command or a commander, without a coherent strategy and without sufficient funds, arms or national determination to pay the price.
A.M. Rosenthal, New York Times columnist

If we declared war, we have thus far lost it.
Bob Graham, Governor of Florida

advance warning of the attacks and had disappeared. Of the twenty-five raids conducted by the middle of August, only a quarter had been successful. They may have diminished cocaine production in Bolivia in the short term, but are unlikely to have made a permanent dent in the trade.

Soldiers set fire to paraffin trenches during a raid on a jungle lab in Colombia.

5
The international response

The trade in drugs, and the misery it causes, have long been recognized as problems that can only be solved by international effort. The United Nations has been involved since 1946, when it established the Commission on Narcotic Drugs, and has been responsible for two international conventions, or agreements. The 1961 Convention on Narcotic Drugs provides for controls over production, manufacture, distribution and availability of drugs derived from opium, and cocaine and marijuana. In 1971, a similar convention was agreed covering synthetic drugs such as the hallucinogens, stimulants and sedatives. The existence of these two conventions means that, in principle at least, the countries who sign are obliged to do all they can to control the trade in drugs.

But agreement in principle is not, of course, sufficient. Recognizing that fact, the U.N. established its Fund for Drug Abuse Control (UNFDAC) in 1971. It is financed entirely by voluntary contributions from governments, and its job is to support individual governments and help to develop plans for tackling the problem. It has so far drawn up plans for Thailand, Pakistan, Bolivia, Peru and Colombia, all countries that are major sources of drugs. Its budget in 1985 was $18.7 million, little enough when compared with the massive sums generated by illegal drug production.

UNFDAC is involved in a variety of different programs. Some seek to improve law enforcement by providing better equipment for drug control. Funds from UNFDAC are often supplemented by aid from Western countries – in Bolivia, for example, the British government has provided about $1 million for equipment and training for the police force as part of an UNFDAC program.

A major effort has been made to eliminate the growing of coca and opium by encouraging the planting of alternative crops. Here UNFDAC efforts have been supplemented by heavy investments from major aid donors such as the United States, Sweden, West Germany and Britain. The money has been spent in providing fruit trees and reliable irrigation to ensure that they grow. In the Buner subdivision of the North West Frontier Province, for example, Pakistani government figures claim that 39,000 fruit trees have been distributed, 3,000 acres irrigated, better animal health systems established, roads built and wells sunk. As a result, the same report says, opium production in Buner stopped in the late 1970s and has not been resumed.

Claims like these make the crop-substitution program look like a great success, but many observers are skeptical. It is doubtful if farmers who were making a bare living out of opium poppies can survive at all by growing fruit, and opposition to the program is increasing. In its annual report to the president on the efforts made by various countries to combat drugs, the U.S. State Department said that the production of opium in Pakistan had risen in 1986 to between 140 and 160 tons, compared with 40 tons in 1984. "This setback was a direct result of the government of Pakistan's failure to respond swiftly when faced with strong opposition by growers to its control policies," the report concludes.

> The farmers of the North West Frontier have been cultivating poppies since time immemorial. They cannot be expected deliberately to starve to death simply in order to please the mighty United States.
> *Professor Sayyid Jafree, President Pakistan Constitutional Law and Public Interests Center*

That was the first report the State Department had issued as a consequence of a law passed

A millet crop in the mountains of Pakistan. The UNFDAC tries to encourage the substitution of food crops for opium poppies.

by Congress requiring the U.S. to reduce by half the economic aid it gives to any country that does not cooperate in fighting drug production. But in spite of its gloomy conclusions about Pakistan's efforts, the State Department did not list Pakistan among those failing to cooperate. Nor did it list Mexico, although it said that a third of the cocaine consumed in the U.S. in 1986 had come through Mexico, and that Mexico was the major single country supplying heroin and marijuana to the United States.

The actual list of countries not cooperating consisted of just three names: Afghanistan, Iran and Syria, none of whom get any aid from the United States anyway. Laos and Lebanon were also named, but because of American "vital interests" they escaped listing. The procedure illustrates quite clearly that in international politics, drugs play a very small role. It seems

that other military, commercial or political relationships are far more important. Not even the nation that has declared war on drugs will do anything to damage those relationships for the sake of controlling drug abuse.

But it would be wrong to portray the battle against drugs as just a cynical exercise. Neither is it simply a clash between the rich world and the economic aims of the poor. Many developing countries now acknowledge that they have a serious problem of their own. Colombia has 600,000 cocaine users, Peru 300,000. There are 500,000 heroin addicts in Thailand, 400–600,000 in Pakistan, 500,000 in India, 110,000 in Malaysia. Even Eastern Europe, where there has been very little attention paid to drug abuse, now recognizes the problem. The Soviet Union's Interior Minister, Alexander Vlasov, said in January 1987 that there were 46,000 registered addicts in the Soviet Union. A senior

Right *This poster in Thailand warns of the dangers of drug addiction.*

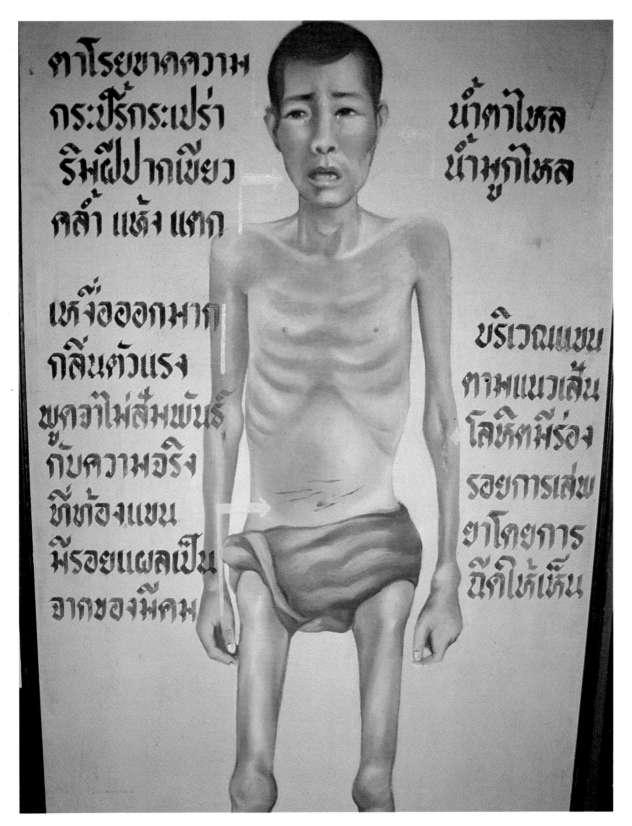

ตาโรยขาดความ
กระปรี้กระเปร่า
ริมฝีปากเขียว
คล้ำ แห้ง แตก

น้ำตาไหล
น้ำหูไหล

เหงื่อออกมาก
กลิ่นตัวแรง
พูดจาไม่สัมพันธ์
กับความจริง
ที่ท้องแขน
มีรอยแผลเป็น
จากของมีคม

บริเวณแขน
ตามแนวเส้น
โลหิตมีร่อง
รอยการเสพ
ยาโดยการ
ฉีดให้เห็น

39

Communist Party official in Moscow has admitted: "We closed our eyes to it for a long time, and we were ashamed to speak about it – but drug abuse is becoming a serious problem."

Many countries are adopting much tougher legislation in an attempt to control drug trafficking. In Malaysia, for example, possession of more than 15 grams of heroin is an offense punishable by death – as a growing number of drug traffickers are discovering. No European country would contemplate such a tough law, though sentencing policy has become noticeably tougher, and new legislation has been passed in the United States, Britain and Italy that makes it possible to confiscate the assets of convicted drug traffickers. The object is to prevent drug traffickers from benefiting from their criminal activities by transferring assets to their wives or associates.

The twelve European Community countries, meeting in London in October 1986, agreed that confiscation of traffickers' assets should be part of a seven-point plan for tackling drug abuse. The other six points included joint intelligence gathering, preparation of reports on drug-producing countries and increased customs surveillance at the Community's external

Sentencing policy for drug-related crimes varies widely around the world. These Westeners are serving up to fifteen years in Bolivian jails for relatively minor offenses.

> In many cases, I think the narcotics smugglers are better equipped than the U.S. government.
> *Jerry Padalino, antidrug official (referring to the increase in narcotics traffic over the Mexican border)*

borders. But there was no mention of a uniform drug enforcement and sentencing policy throughout the Community, which had been recommended earlier that month by a committee of the European Parliament.

The reason is that one Community country – the Netherlands – is still operating a much more liberal sentencing policy than the rest. The Dutch have stuck to a policy that was widely followed in Europe in the 1960s but has now been abandoned: that the criminalization of drugs does little to control their use, and associating drugs and crime creates more problems than it solves. According to this view, addicts should be provided with drugs quite legally by their doctors, so they do not have to resort to crime or prostitution to finance their addiction. In the Netherlands, although it is technically a crime to own or traffic in heroin, cocaine or marijuana, the Public Prosecutions Department does not usually prosecute addicts found in possession of drugs, and the sale of marijuana on a small scale is allowed to go on undisturbed. This has made Amsterdam something of a haven for drug addicts, but the Dutch authorities claim that it has real benefits.

The use of marijuana has actually declined since the policy was introduced in 1976, it says, while it has been rising in West Germany. But the same is certainly not true of heroin, the use of which has risen rapidly in the Netherlands, as elsewhere in Europe, over the past decade. The Dutch policy raises strong passions. One British member of the European Parliament calls Amsterdam "the cesspit of Europe.

Right *Some people claim that unemployment among young people is a major cause of drug abuse in the West. Youngsters may turn to drugs out of boredom and resentment.*

41

The poison from there has spread around," he says. "I believe the Dutch government ought to be looking at their consciences." But Dutch sociologist Eddy Engelsman, who has advised the Dutch government on its drug policies, rejects the call for a uniform sentencing policy in Europe. "We find it strange" he says, "waging drug crusades. We do take drug problems seriously, and we have creative, new ideas about them. Now, what we are doing has become unthinkable."

In fact, the Dutch policies are not so much new as old. Throughout the 1950s and 1960s British drug policy was to provide registered addicts with drugs on prescription, as a way of ensuring that addiction remained a medical rather than a criminal problem. It appeared to work comparatively well when addiction was still a fairly small problem, but it did have some serious drawbacks. Addicts often sold some of the drugs they were prescribed, spreading the habit. It did not always result in addicts leading a more stable life; many experimented with other drugs as well as the heroin, or heroin substitute, they had been prescribed. And it tended to confirm in the minds of addicts that their addiction was incurable – that there was no way they could ever survive without drugs.

It was for reasons like these that British policy changed in the late 1970s, largely due to the urging of the doctors who ran the Drug Dependency Units. There are now very few addicts who are prescribed "maintenance" doses of heroin or its substitute, methadone. The policy applied is one of abstinence. All that survives of the liberal policy is a marked reluctance to prosecute those who possess small quantities of drugs. It is recognized that there is little point in filling the prisons with those who are themselves victims of drug addiction while the real criminals – the traders and dealers – go free.

In principle, the new policy must be right. It is surely better to cure addicts of their obsession with drugs, rather than confirm them in a life of addiction by prescribing maintenance doses. Unfortunately, though, abstinence is a very difficult policy to follow, particularly when most addicts are treated as outpatients. Between treatments they are free to return to their homes and the environments in which they

became addicts in the first place. Experts in drug addiction believe that this method is unlikely to succeed. They prefer inpatient treatment in which the addict stays in a clinic for several months, taking part in a busy time-table of lectures, discussions and therapy. Such clinics do exist, but they are very expensive – $1,500 a week or more. A complete course involving some months of inpatient treatment, followed by another eighteen months or so of outpatient treatment, can cost up to $20,000 in one of the more successful American treatment centers. Even so, it is no guarantee of recovery, and some patients do relapse, even after completing the whole program.

Since cure is so expensive and difficult, most governments are now putting a lot of effort into prevention. In the United States, President Reagan and First Lady Nancy Reagan have been active in waging war on drugs. Congress recently passed a federal anti-drug-abuse act that made funds available to educate young people about drugs. "Our goal," stated President Reagan, "is a drug-free generation in the United States." In 1985, a group of parents in Oakland, California, began to organize "Just Say No" clubs, and by 1986, there were already 10,000 clubs across the country.

It is almost impossible to measure the effectiveness of such campaigns. Even if addiction continues to rise, one cannot know whether it might have risen even faster without the television campaign and the posters. There is, too, the danger that by drawing attention to drugs you may even make them seem attractive in a perverse way. Anything that adults disapprove of so violently must be worth a try – that is certainly one possible reaction from some young people.

One thing is quite clear. Drug addiction is such a complex problem, and the trade in drugs so difficult to prevent, that it must be tackled simultaneously at every level: production, trafficking, dealing, prevention, treatment and rehabilitation. No single approach can provide a solution, but taken together they may begin to have a perceptible effect.

Right *This poster was part of the British government's antiheroin campaign in 1985.*

43

Glossary

Abstinence   Stopping the taking drugs altogether.

Active ingredient   The component of a mixture that is responsible for its effect.

Assets   Money and property.

Commodities   Goods that can be traded.

Customs   A tax on imports or exports; a control point for goods entering or leaving a country.

Customs officers   Officials who control the import and export of goods.

Derivative   A derivative of a substance is made from that substance.

Drugs baron   A rich and powerful drug dealer.

Euphoric   Exciting, joyful.

European Community   An economic and political association of twelve European countries.

European Parliament   Parliament of the European Community.

Excise   A tax on goods produced for the home market.

Folk remedy   A traditional method of medical treatment.

Hallucination   The experience of sensing (e.g. seeing or hearing) things that are not really present.

Hallucinogen   A substance that causes hallucinations.

Hedonistic   Pleasure-seeking.

Illicit   Illegal.

Irrigation   The process of supplying of water to dry regions.

Latin America   The Spanish-and Portuguese-speaking countries of America.

Legislation   Laws.

Legitimate   Legal.

Mercenary   A soldier who is paid to fight for a foreign country.

Middlemen   Traders who buy goods from the producers and sell them to the retailers.

Narcotic   A drug such as opium or morphine that reduces pain, but may be addictive.

Prohibition   A policy, practiced in the United States from 1919 to 1932, of forbidding the manufacture, sale and consumption of alcoholic drinks.

Psychoanalysis   A method of psychological treatment that emphasizes the importance of the unconscious mind.

Ratified   Approved.

Rehabilitation   Readapting to society.

Retailer   Someone who sells goods directly to the public.

Sedative   A drug that has a calming effect.

Solvent   A liquid that dissolves other substances.

Stimulant   A drug that increases physiological activity (e.g. heart rate) and produces a feeling of excitement.

United Nations   An international organization formed in 1945 to promote international peace and cooperation.

Versailles Treaty   The major peace treaty that ended World War I.

Volatile   Evaporating easily.

Books to read

Mind Drugs by Margaret O. Hyde (Dodd, Mead, 1986)
Addiction: Its Causes, Problems, and Treatment by Gilda Berger (Watts, 1982)
Drugs and Society by Richard A. Hawley (Walker, 1988)
International Drug Traffic by Edward F. Dolan, Jr. (Watts, 1985)
The Heroin Trail by Nigel Hawkes (Watts, 1986)
The Marijuana Question by Helen C. Jones and Paul W. Lovinger (Dodd, Mead, 1985)

Picture Acknowledgments

Camera Press 6 (Martin Patternotte), 11 (David Hoffman), 16 (David Lomax), 31 (David Lomax), 34 (The Times), 40 (David Lomax); DHSS 43; Mary Evans Picture Library 13; Sally & Richard Greenhill 8; Hutchison Library 17, 20, 22, 36; Tony Morrison 21; Christine Osborne Pictures frontispiece, 19, 25, 26, 32, 33, 39; Rex Features cover; Frank Spooner Pictures 9 (A. Borrel), 15 (Richard Tomkins), 24, 28 (Piero Guerrini), 41 (arkell-Spooner); Topham Picture Library 7, 10, 23, 27, 29, 30, 35, 38; ZEFA 14; maps on page 18 by Malcolm Walker.

Further Information

Just Say No Clubs
1777 N. California Blvd, Suite 200
Walnut Creek, CA 94596

A nationwide series of young student
clubs dedicated to combating and
eliminating drug abuse among students.

War on Drugs
5456 Lake Avenue
Sanford, FL 32771

Individiuals interested in combating the
use of illegal drugs by eliminating
their distribution through drug pushers.

Narcotics Educational Foundation of
    America
5055 Sunset Boulevard
Los Angeles, CA 90027

This organization provides information
about narcotics and other drugs to warn
youths and adults about the dangers of
drug abuse. It helps produce film and TV
programs about drugs and distributes
printed materials.

Index